Roger Coote and Diana Bentley

A Journey by Plane

Firefly

We are going on a plane.
This is the airport.

We have to walk through
a tunnel to get into the plane.

We sit in our seats and
fasten our safety belts.
The engines are getting louder.
Soon we shall be off.

Oh! We're up in the air.
The earth is tipping over!

There are clouds all around us.
They always look so far away but
our plane goes through them.

Here is our meal.
The food is all in little dishes.

Now we are flying through a storm.
The stewardess has come to
fasten our safety belts again.
The storm is exciting.
And a bit frightening too!

We walk down the plane.
It has lots of seats.
Here is one of the
toilets at the back.
How small it is.

The pilot has invited us
into the cabin.
How can you fly a plane when
all you can see is sky?

A person who flies must
be very brave.
When I grow up
I'm going to
fly every kind of
flying machine.

Look! A small flap has
come out of the wing.
The sound of the engines is changing.
We are starting to go down!

At the airport, the people in the control tower are talking to our pilot.
They are telling him that it is safe to land.

The plane is landing.
We have had an exciting day and
we will never forget our first
journey by plane.

Notes for adults

Children who come to school already knowing how a book 'works' have a great deal of knowledge that will help them to make the entry into reading much easier. It is far more important to share a book with a child than to try to teach him/her to read. These books aim to introduce very young children to the world around them.

Before reading this book talk about the pictures on the cover. What does your child think the book is about? Talk about the title and point to the words. Tell him/her that all books are written by authors and often illustrated by a different person. Show them the names of the author and illustrator.

Before reading the story look through the book together and talk about the illustrations. Encourage your child to tell his/her own story to the pictures. This important pre-reading skill helps children to develop an understanding of story that is essential to reading.

Do let your child hold the book and give him/her time to look at the pictures before talking about them. Adults often rush in with questions far too soon.

REMEMBER when looking at the pictures there is no 'right' or 'wrong' guess. Accept what your child suggests and add your own ideas. You will be bringing much more knowledge to the pictures but s/he may surprise you.

After reading the book let your child explore the book on his/her own. S/he may want to return to a favourite picture, retell the story to a special toy, or just turn the pages pretending to be a reader. A joy in books comes from being allowed to use them as the reader wishes and not necessarily as a parent would have them do.

Discussion points

Talking about the illustrations will help your child to get more from the story. Here are some suggestions for things to discuss. The numbers refer to the pages on which the illustrations appear.

4/5 Look at all the people in the airport. Where do you think they are going? Can you see the clock?

7 How do you think the children get on to the plane? Do you think they are excited?

9 Can you see the seat belt? Why has the little boy shut his eyes?

11 What can the little girl see out of the window?

12/13 What is the plane going through?

15 What have the children been given to eat?

19 What are the children looking at?

21 Can you see the pilot? What is he showing the children?

22/23 How many flying machines can you see? Which would you like to fly in?

25 What can the children see out of the window?

28/29 The plane is landing. Would you like to go on a plane journey?